WRITE ACROSS CANADA

Mapping the Country in 19 Chapters

Commissioned by

the
ottawa
INTERNATIONAL
writers
festival
www.writersfest.com

Illustrated by Drew Kennickell

NIGHTWOOD EDITIONS

Roberts Creek, BC

Nightwood Editions
RR#22, 3692 Beach Avenue
Roberts Creek, BC
V0N 2W2
www.nightwoodeditions.com

Cover illustration and design by Drew Kennickell
Edited for the house by Silas White
Printed and bound in Canada

Nightwood Editions acknowledges financial support from the Government of Canada through the Canada Council for the Arts; and from the Province of British Columbia through the British Columbia Arts Council.

The Canada Council for the Arts Since 1957 | Le Conseil des Arts du Canada Depuis 1957

British Columbia Arts Council
Supported by the Province of British Columbia

Library and Archives Canada Cataloguing in Publication

Write across Canada : mapping the country in 19 chapters / commissioned by the Ottawa International Writers Festival.

ISBN 0-88971-199-2

I. Ottawa International Writers Festival.

PS8323.C35W75   2004C813'.6   C2004-904492-3

Contents

INTRODUCTION
Peter Schneider   9

Chapter 1
ST. JOHN'S, NEWFOUNDLAND
Michael Winter   13

Chapter 2
HALIFAX, NOVA SCOTIA
Donna Morrissey   17

Chapter 3
NORTH RUSTICO, PRINCE EDWARD ISLAND
Lesley-Anne Bourne   21

Chapter 4
MONCTON, NEW BRUNSWICK
Herménégilde Chiasson   27

Chapter 5
FREDERICTON, NEW BRUNSWICK
Mark Anthony Jarman   31

Chapter 6.
QUEBEC CITY, QUEBEC
Nalini Warriar   35

Chapter 7
MONTREAL, QUEBEC
Tess Fragoulis   39

Chapter 8
OTTAWA, ONTARIO
Alan Cumyn   43

Chapter 9
KINGSTON, ONTARIO
Helen Humphreys   47

Chapter 10
TORONTO, ONTARIO
Sheila Heti   *51*

Chapter 11
WINNIPEG, MANITOBA
Uma Parameswaran   *55*

Chapter 12
SASKATOON, SASKATCHEWAN
Arthur Slade   *61*

Chapter 13
REGINA, SASKATCHEWAN
Dianne Warren   *67*

Chapter 14
EDMONTON, ALBERTA
Thomas Wharton   *71*

Chapter 15
CALGARY, ALBERTA
paulo da costa   *75*

Chapter 16
FORT SMITH, NORTHWEST TERRITORIES
Richard Van Camp   *81*

Chapter 17
**MCRAE MOTOR INN AND RESTAURANT, JUST SOUTH
OF WHITEHORSE, YUKON TERRITORY**
Ivan E. Coyote   *89*

Chapter 18
VANCOUVER, BRITISH COLUMBIA
Steven Galloway   *93*

Chapter 19
VICTORIA, BRITISH COLUMBIA
Bill Gaston   *97*

CONTRIBUTORS   *103*

INTRODUCTION

Peter Schneider

What to make of this shaggy-dog story, this Franken-stein's monster of a tale? As a literary sub-genre, chain fiction has its roots in parody, and by nature it is a pastiche. Here, we have a fresh take on the road novel, given a Canadian spin and cobbled together by nineteen writers who take delight in subverting expectations and tripping one another up—as a literary performance, this story is an extended series of pratfalls, yet somehow it is also unexpectedly moving. Given the predominantly serious nature of most literary fiction in this country, this is a rare opportunity to witness some of our brightest lights at play, tweaking national myths with ingenuity and a genuine affection that shines through in the end. Along the way, issues of cultural identity, gender, region-al isolation, addiction and personal taste are debated—

sometimes explicitly, but more often between the lines. As an exercise, this cumulative story of a misbegotten cross-country love affair is a formalist's nightmare—crucial plot developments are negated, the narration is of a variety referred to by academics as 'unreliable,' and there is no single, consistent point of view. If there is a connecting thread running throughout the tale, it is a begrudging acknowledgment that Canada is an idea larger than its constituent parts—that a country is made up of specific places and regions, with their accompanying rivalries and misunderstandings, and that each part is essential to the whole.

No parameters were set on subject matter or on style—each writer was asked to provide a short chapter of six hundred words within forty-eight hours of receiving the work-in-progress, in order to keep things moving cross-country, and to simulate the vivid impressions and spontaneity of a road trip. This might explain the fevered quality of Olivia and Bruce's adventures, though the omnipresent bottle of Bushmills whiskey, and its travelling companion, the CD by roots musician and quick-change artist extraordinaire Will Oldham, are also possible sources of the story's delirium.

Each participant was asked to situate their segment of the narrative in a favourite place in their home city or region, a real-life location that would anchor the tale and give it colour. Michael Winter, launching the story in Newfoundland, made an iconic choice—St. John's Harbour. Environments both natural and man-made follow one another—it shouldn't be too surprising that Bruce and Olivia's cross-country odyssey also serves as a guide to bars, restaurants and truck stops worth visiting when passing through, for the writing life has always thrived on animated conversation and camaraderie. Other destinations are more offbeat, none more so than Alan Cumyn's deployment of the Mer Bleu, a unique wetland ecosystem kilometres away from Parliament Hill, to represent Ottawa. As the story begins in the Atlantic Ocean, it concludes in the Pacific, with Bill Gaston gently nudging our fated couple into the Strait of Juan de Fuca and beyond.

This aquatic symmetry is Gaston's grace note, indicative of his attentive style and dexterity with the ending of a story. In between the calm blue oceans, however, all is not peaceful. Bruce and Olivia meet, part ways, and come together again, always seeming to be on the cusp of a sudden quarrel, yet continuing to reconcile, to work things out, as they head west. Each chapter announces itself as a piquant set piece, whether we are in the hands of Helen Humphreys explaining Kingston's singular population mix of university students and ex-convicts, or with Sheila Heti crawling the hip sidewalks of Toronto's Queen Street. By the time we arrive in Winnipeg, the lovers have parted, and it is up to Uma Parameswaran to sit in the karmic penalty box with Bruce, wittily introducing post-modern consciousness and metafictional byplay before passing the puck to Arthur Slade in Saskatoon.

Inexorably, even painfully, the pair makes their journey. Thomas Wharton, picking things up in Edmonton, has Olivia ask, "What's the point anymore? Everyone knows the story's over by the time it crosses the Ontario border." This jab at the centre of the country is perhaps understandable in context—nearing the end of the line, Bruce and Olivia have been through much drama, including two pregnancies and a handful of attempts at quitting cigarettes. An attentive reader can sense the writers becoming restive with their collective creation, so much so that Dianne Warren, in Regina, opts to make them passive bystanders in an enigmatic vignette beside the highway. The chapters continue to come in giddy succession, as Bruce and Olivia head north and west, acquiring subplots and displaying new wrinkles and a few writerly grey hairs. The ridiculous is rendered sublime, rescued repeatedly by the individual voice of a Canadian writer rising to the occasion. The stitching may be crooked, but this is one beautiful, crazy quilt.

Peter Schneider is an Ottawa journalist. A former book reviewer for the *Ottawa XPress*, Peter is currently the managing editor of *Embassy: Diplomacy This Week*.

Chapter 1

Michael Winter

ST. JOHN'S, NEWFOUNDLAND

I met Olivia in St. John's Harbour. I was diving, my first scuba dive. When you're underwater, everything is imbued with significance. Olivia's legs, the blue lobster with his back arched, the black humpback that we had swum beside. The slow motion aspect makes you feel like you're in a movie. This is important, remember this. Olivia beckoned me. She had surfaced and I saw her hand plunge into the lid of the sea and wave me up. I came up. I broke the surface. I grasped her hand and looked into her face. Through the tempered glass of my mask things looked wonky, larger than life. I had breathed underwater for the first time and my partner, a stranger until this buddy dive, was Olivia, and I realized I had torn through some dimension and was falling in love with her.

She was oblivious to this love. She drove a pickup and smoked Dunhills and listened to Will Oldham. She would screw me that night but she was impervious to love. She was enjoying herself. She said, Help me off with this, will you?

She was leaning against the back of her open tailgate. The sun sinking over the arterial road trickled across the neoprene of her wetsuit. She wanted me to peel off her wetsuit. I grabbed the black wet fabric and tugged at her thighs as she smoked.

That, she said. Wasn't that something.

We had swum down to a recently discovered Spanish galleon. It was as if we had descended back in time five hundred years. There was a relationship between depth and history—you always had to dig for ruins. Olivia lived on the road up to Signal Hill. We packed our regulators and tanks and flotation vests in a black plastic tub in the back of her truck. She wore earrings that reminded me of Barcelona. We drove to the top of the city listening to Will Oldham. She had a guitar and she had written one beautiful song. Olivia was tender and had a face that would go through a lot.

There was a bottle of Bushmills in her glove compartment. She had two Duralex glasses and ice in a cooler. She poured me a drink. We sat on the hood of her GMC and looked out on the city we both loved, that had nurtured us and taught us that small things can be fruitful and an antidote to the big life. The city spread out from the harbour apron like many rows of teeth and the light on the renovated church shone out the Harbour Narrows to guide ships into port. We drank our whiskey and leaned against each other, the ice cubes touching my lip as we stared at the sea which held a vast green and white sculpture of an iceberg, and a lonely humpback curved its back towards us. It was easy to feel like that humpback was in us. That we were making that humpback sing. But it was Will Oldham and the city that were telling us to live. Olivia was a woman who, after she took me home and we made love, would leave her sunglasses on the stove and they melted into the drip pan on her back burner.

I have to go soon, she said.

I listened to this.

You can come, she said. If you behave.

I'm in love with you, I said.

I don't want to hear that. I'm too young for that.

She had a booking on the Argentia ferry. It was fourteen hours to North Sydney. She had a tent and some poems to write and I could come with her if I behaved and split the gas.

Chapter 2

Donna Morrissey

HALIFAX, NOVA SCOTIA

Olivia's GMC lumbered into a parking spot in front of the Lord Nelson Hotel in Halifax and I gratefully shoved open the door, letting out a cloud of cigarette smoke, the nasal twang of Will Oldham, and my own cramped self. Olivia got out on the other side, grounding out her latest Dunhill.

"You know this city, right?" she asked. "Can we get to the Busker Festival from here? Sounds like a lot of fun, all of them acts and people from all over the world."

I shrug. Somewhere on the ferry I had turned to sap

over this woman, and was searching for a more intimate atmosphere to awaken that oblivious heart to the wonder of love—my love. In front of us sprawled the public gardens, sixteen acres of exotic flowers, shrubbery, trees, birds—a bouquet of color and scent. "Let's walk," I say, leading her through a set of ornate gates.

She pulled back, looking around skeptically. "I—I'm not sure—"

"It's a Victorian garden—you'll love it. See Egeria over there?"

"Huh?"

"The statue over there, atop the Corinthian column—see the water babies riding the serpents? The figure above them, rising out of the basin, is Egeria. She was turned into a fountain when she tried to hide in the forest after her husband's death. Have you ever thought of love, Olivia?"

"I wouldn't *die* for it," said Olivia.

I led her towards Ceres, Diana and Flora. "Flora was married to the west wind," I said.

"Must've been turbulent. Look, I'm not sure I want to be here—is this—" she hesitated, glancing around with a discomfited look. "Is this the Public Gardens?"

"Yup. Been here since the 1800s—set up so's the poor as well as the rich could have a place to sit. Nice, hey?"

"Yeah, real nice," said Olivia. "And now let's just cut through this corner and get the hell out of here."

She started walking real fast, pulling a Dunhill out of her pocket, and striking a match. I chased after her.

"Fine, you wanna go, let's go, but this is the quickest route to downtown," I said, taking her arm. Surprisingly, she let me lead her back in the other direction, past the war memorial, around the rhododendrons, and beside a large pond littered with ducks and swans.

"Griffins Pond," I said to her, reading from a plaque as we passed by. "Hey, isn't that your mother's name— Griffin? Jeezes, see this," and I lagged behind, reading out the rest of the plaque—named after an Irishman who was hanged for murder—isn't your mother Irish? Come to think of it, didn't she live around here, somewhere? Olivia!"

She'd walked on, almost running, puffs of smoke from her Dunhill like little clouds dispersing behind her. "Olivia, what the hell, wait up—"

"I like things that move," she said angrily as I caught up with her, "not dead."

"Hey, okay," I said as she shoved out through a set of gates, heading towards where her truck was parked. I followed. "What's wrong?" I asked.

She turned to me, her mouth twisted with anger, yet her eyes soft, luminous behind their veil of tears.

"I'm outta here, buddy," she said, voice quavering. "You want a drive to PEI, you can come. But talk to me no more about the dead or your stupid myths. Alright?"

She dug her keys out of her pocket, dropping them. I picked them up.

"I can drive," I said quietly.

Without speaking, she climbed into the passenger seat. Slamming the door shut, she cranked up Will Oldham, making more talk impossible

Chapter 3

Lesley-Anne Bourne

NORTH RUSTICO, PRINCE EDWARD ISLAND

The closest I'd come to saying his name had been when I called him "buddy." I had trouble with guys named Bruce—a track record, and the name was so common, wasn't it? In the truck that evening, I made myself take a run at it.

"Bruce, I want to go to North Rustico, first—I don't care what happens after."

"Okay, O. Fine by me."

We were on the bridge. The suspended moments between here and there.

You'd think the path would be straight, wouldn't you, I thought. A fixed link—spanning past and present Bruces—should be straight as an arrow, shouldn't it? Flat as a pancake. What other clichés are there? Still as glass, lakes were that, weren't they? Calm as glass?

A glass bridge. How beautiful. How simple.

But we weren't dealing with small bodies of water, were we? We were headed for ocean. Away from elegant Victorian gardens, designed and contained, floral architecture. Heading for possible riptides.

I tried to say Bruce a few times in my head, so it wouldn't stick in my throat so much, so it wouldn't make me think of fish bones, so it wouldn't make me picture the wharf, so that it wouldn't make me get somewhere before I actually got there. I was trying to keep going before I was gone. I tried to stay with the GOING part, rather than jump ahead to the GOTTEN TO part. In weak attempts to end my tobacco addiction (Bushmills and Will Oldham could stay), lately I'd been reading too many books on Buddhism. I'd been working on living in the present—and I was proving to be lousy at it. Buddhism. Diving. Stick your head into the mouth of fear. Or was it desire? Buddhism. Buddhism. Buddy. Buddy.

Bruce, Bruce, Bruce.

"What?"

NICE, I thought, don't say things for real, you idiot, Bolivia.

"Bolivia?" asked Bruce, trying to refold a map which I had previously made fit the glove compartment—made it fit in a hurry or anger, it appeared, and the paper accordion smelled like cigarettes and Bushmills.

Bolivia had been my secret name since childhood for when I screwed up. And I worried I may have screwed up—I should have known better for godsake—after all, his name was Bruce.

"VERY NICE it," I said, and remembered how my father, retired from engineering and planning, but not really, had said the first time we drove the bridge on our way to the north shore, that the structure was curved and elevated here and there to prevent hypnotism. I didn't know if he was joking or serious—and anyway, at the present moment (Thank you Buddha, Buddy, or Bruce), it didn't seem relevant. It was already too late, wasn't it?

"What?"

"Sorry, Bruce, I have a habit of talking out loud."

"Is there any other kind?" he asked, laughing.

Beware his laugh, Buddha said. Or was that my intuition?

"I meant to say THINKING, I said. I have a habit of THINKING out loud."

I'm getting used to his name, I thought. Oh-oh.

"Oh," said Bruce.

Just head there, I told myself, making sure this time

it was silently. Making sure I was following the bridge, as the other side's red banks grew bigger, and redder, reminding me of a sponge lobster I'd had as a girl, which grew in seconds when tossed in a tub full of bubbles.

Lobster, a labyrinth of traps on the wharf, the sour-salt-wet wood evening air. Tonight's. Too late, I thought, I'm there.

I couldn't tell if it was resignation or surrender. This was often tricky, I thought, especially where Bruces (What WAS the plural—Bruce-i? Like octopi?) were concerned. But I was already there, with Bruce, and could feel the heaved and also collapsing-in-places pavement beside the wharf—pavement fossilized and containing wind, salt, rain, sun, ice, fear, hope, confusion, love. All the abstracts.

Very VERY NICE, I thought while still driving AND still seeing tail lights bending the highway to the north shore, and the harbour that would be there as always—both at once. NOW and THEN.

Just beyond the boats (*Bob's Girl*, *Shady Lady*, *Misty*, *Black Beauty* and more), the boardwalk—so tidy, so new, such an urban path for such a longstanding harbour. But somehow I thought it fit—and loved walking it at night, with the wind—wasn't there always wind, unleashed and wagging. The boardwalk beside the harbour, edging it, and calmly lining the new estates—brick and vinyl—as if to keep them safely on the other side, no leaching, no contaminating the water. The sheltered water, the flip side of the water you could hear nearby, open.

Don't think about open water, I told myself. It's even more the future. Think more presently, protected water, stay with the boardwalk, Buddha Bolivia. The boardwalk along the harbour, past Kevin and Aldera's, and Donnie's music parties, past the other houses, and then down the road to the kayak rental place.

Their sign, Bolivia always thought, screamed their name as a command—GET OUT.

And then turning to the lighthouse.

Like a heart.

A heart? Bolivia, how clichéd is that?

"Is what?"

Sorry, Bruce, I said in my head, and meant it, because I knew what was coming. I've been down this boardwalk before, around the lighthouse and the way it waits there, shining, for distress and more, day and night, but especially at night. Lighthouses just stand there, waiting for us to come to them. Waiting for us to trample dunes. Grass and sand. Heart and head. What else is there?

"Listen," Bruce, I said. "You're gonna love me."

I could tell by the expression on his oncoming lights-lit face that I didn't say, "love IT." I'd meant to.

Chapter 4

Herménégilde Chiasson

MONCTON, NEW BRUNSWICK

Napoleon wrote somewhere that in love the only victory is to escape. For Bruce love was still the best solution to end one's anxiety. Crossing the Confederation Bridge with him had seemed to Olivia like one of those irrational decisions that she was prone to, something like leaving the solid ground to move unto a small continent called an island. They had slept together trying to make sense of what had been happening during those hectic days. The urge of being in love, the idea of finding a way to fit that in one's life. And suddenly the only solution that made sense for her. Escape.

Moving with angel-like lightness she slipped out of the bed and drifted through the room gathering the few things she had left floating around and with robot-like precision, opened the door and moved across the parking lot into the truck, leaving Bruce behind. Sound asleep in the hazy quietness of that foggy morning. That endless road within the concrete blinding wall and the idea that kept coming to her mind that the longest bridge in the world is still the one that separates woman from man.

And now she was driving along as usual with no-where to go except following the road that seemed to know better than her where she was heading to. Was it those books on Buddhism? The notion that the road stands still while going somewhere. She didn't know. All she knew was that she was driving away from him, away from his voice, from his dreams, from that way he had of reading out loud, from wanting her for him, for him only. She felt like she was crossing the ocean, looking downwards from way high to some small island that looked like his body.

The Zen says that all life is suffering caused by desires that you have to eliminate in order to regain conscience. Maybe that's what she was driving away from: Desire. She said the word out loud. It sounded like a foghorn. Loud with the *d* propped strongly on the teeth, the *z* escaping from under the gums and then the rest of the word lost in the echo of the throat. She remembered the taste of his mouth, the movement of his jaws around her lips and that tension that he injected into her whole body to make every nerve totally alive. Totally herself. Desire. It became a song when she started to expand it like a mantra.

Leaving the Confederation Bridge behind she took the road for Moncton driving along those Acadian villages that were emerging from the vanishing fog. She put on Will Oldham. She had almost forgotten about him but when he sang "New Gypsy," she thought he was singing just for her. Some kind of command performance. The whole truck came alive.

She stopped for gas in Cap-Pelé and got a coffee from one of those doubtful machines, asked about directions to the young man at the gas pump and got underway for Moncton. She arrived there at nine. She drove along Main and took a left on Church Street, there is one in every city and she always felt it had been her lucky street. There were three churches to choose from and she parked her truck in front of St. Bernard's and decided to walk around town for a while.

Joe Moka Café. She thought that might be a good place to have a real coffee and besides the word "café" always had for her a continental flavour but more than that she thought that this might be a good place to meet some French people, the legendary Acadians whom she had heard about in Newfoundland. She felt some affinity with them. Their isolation that had made them like the inhabitants of an island she was driving away from.

Chapter 5

Mark Anthony Jarman

FREDERICTON, NEW BRUNSWICK

We wake up beside a big river, fathoms of appled sunlight filling the ripples.

"How did you find me?"

"Where are we?"

"Freddy Beach."

"Last I remember we were in Moncton drinking at the Pump House with some Acadian dude who claimed he was the next Lieutenant-Governor of New Brunswick."

"Yeah, and I'm the Queen of the Nile."

"Got both kidneys?"

"Check."

White sailboats bob at their moorings on the river as one water skier is pulled past and a Sea-Doo carves wild circles and smashes through its own waves.

"Be nice to get out on the river."

"That it would."

"Hey kid, yeah you with the crutches. Can we borrow your little raft? We'll bring it right back. Scout's honour."

It's hot and sunny but the water is freezing. We clamber in and drift on the river past the lighthouse and the Cathedral and the Stroll and past Fredericton's one squeegee kid (soon to give up). We float under the iron railroad bridge and past the big houses on Waterloo Row where Benedict Arnold had a land grant from Mad King George.

So close to downtown and yet we spy an osprey chasing after fish and watch an eagle take down a duck. Two prehistoric herons croak loudly as they burst out of trees right above our head.

"Arr matey."

"Ya ever been ta sea, Billy?"

A small black dog barks at us from shore, then leaps in the water.

"Intruder alert."

"Hey dog, stay away from our good ship."

Three boys on shore call to their dog: "Vic, stop. Vic, come here. Vic, don't bite their raft."

"Get that durn critter away from us."

Vic's tidy teeth sink into our noble but ill-fated vessel.

"Captain, we've taken a hit bad below the waterline, we're listing to starboard, we're heeling, we're taking on water, we have road-trip B.O. real bad, we lost our jib and mainsheet."

"We never had a jib."

"The port bilge pumps can't keep up, Captain, any more and she'll blow!"

"I'm going down with my ship."

We stand up in one foot of water.

A police car cruises up, driving right on the lush grass alongside the river.

"You're not from around here, are you? Thought you might be smuggling black market fiddleheads from the north side to the south side. Getting to be a bit of a problem here."

The *Daily Gleaner* reporter is happy that he has tomorrow's front page: Dog Bites Raft, Prevents Tragic Drowning.

The dog has no comment but at supper one of the boys will slip him a pizza crust and say, "Good Vic."

The police are called away to a 10-50: someone hit a mailbox and is being set upon by a crowd of indignant retirees who had just finished painting a nice picture of a rather regal woodpecker on said mailbox. Things are hopping in Freddy Beach.

All this talk of fiddleheads makes us hungry. We sell the Will Oldham CDs at Backstreet Records and on the truck's engine we cook up some fiddlehead greens with butter and vinegar and pepper and Tabasco and add some snow crabs from the Acadian shore.

Then we climb the green stairs to the Tap Room deck for pints of Picaroons Bitter, for a road trip is thirsty work. A couple is necking in the washroom. People at the next table speak French. We should check out La Belle Province. Locals give us directions.

"Turn where the railroad track used to be; you can't miss it."

"I tell ya boys, that new highway's some slick."

"Watch for moose though."

"You be careful driving up Suicide Alley."

The hockey arena, the swimming pool, the college dorms, the Stalinist hotel, the art gallery with the big Dali: everything we pass is named after Lord Beaverbrook.

We throw out the Dunhills; no more smoking.

"Lips that touch coffin nails shall never touch mine."

We drive west into the sun, past The Cabin Restaurant where there are tasty home fries and a jukebox on every table. We drive into the light that bathes us.

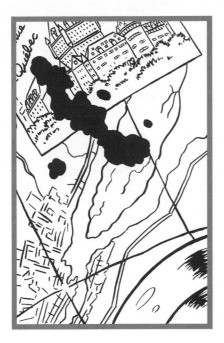

Chapter 6

Nalini Warriar

QUEBEC CITY, QUEBEC

"So, La Belle Province?" Olivia asked as they headed towards the highway.

"Yep," he replied. "And step on it, woman. Got to get me some poutine real soon."

So she stepped on it.

In Quebec City, she drove along boulevard Champlain, past the winding cobbled rue Petit-Champlain and found a spot for her pickup near the river. As she got out, she heard it calling to her as it had done many times before. She pulled out her last Dunhill, lit it and took a deep puff. Tourists in straw hats strolled with cameras slung around their necks. There was the smell of fish and fries in the air. Flowers spilled from window boxes. Quebec City looked like a grand old European dame.

The river got louder. Olivia saw the ferry, *Louis Jolliet*, pull away from the pier. People crowded the railings while children cried to each other in loud voices. Olivia turned her back on it and, taking his hand, she dragged him up Côte de la Montagne. When they reached the top of the road, they took the stairs to the Château Frontenac.

On the promenade Dufferin, she leaned her arms on the railing and looked out to the river. It stretched out in front of her, white sails dotting the calm surface. The Île d'Orléans swelled like a sleeping monster. She craned her neck to get a better glimpse of the bridge that connected the island to the mainland. A grumble in her stomach reminded her that it was time to eat.

"Come let's get a bite to eat," she said.

"Where?" he asked.

"There's a bistro in the Château where they make the most delicious club sandwiches."

"Do they have poutine?"

"Don't know. We could get that later if they don't have it. At the Ashton on Saint-Jean."

"Righto."

After they'd eaten—he didn't get his poutine—they

took the million stairs up to the Plains of Abraham. She had to stop to catch her breath now and then.

That evening, at the Manoir d'Auteuil after he'd fallen asleep, she made her way once again to the promenade Dufferin. The river was now a dark gap of inky nothingness below her. On the south shore, she saw the lights on the ferry flickering as it made one more trip from Lévis.

Head down, she stared at the thick planks of wood beneath her feet as she walked. She wished she'd thought of bringing the Dunhills with her. Anyway it was probably better this way. She'd been thinking of quitting for some time now.

Suddenly she heard a sound she hadn't heard in a long time. Not since Jimmy and she had parted.

There it was again!

A groan surely.

She stopped in her tracks and listened.

She hesitated. Three years with Jimmy had taught her not to interfere.

And then she came upon them. There was the sound of a scuffle. They saw her at the same time. Two were standing over the body of a third man. As soon as they saw her, their sneakers flashed briefly and then they were gone.

With bated breath, Olivia bent over the lying man. A trickle of blood ran from his temple, across the cheek and pooled on the ground. His eyes were closed. Her first instinct told her to run as far away as she could.

And she followed it. It had never failed her. That was the reason she was still alive.

When her heart stopped hammering, when she stopped listening for the sirens, she went back to the river's side.

"I know," she whispered to the St. Lawrence. "I know I should have called the police. But I couldn't. You understand that, don't you?"

Chapter 7

Tess Fragoulis

MONTREAL, QUEBEC

By the time they reached Montreal, Olivia was done with company, done with talking, done with listening to him opine, complain and moon over her. Even the one Oldham CD she'd refused to part with at Backstreet Records was getting on her nerves. She popped it out of the player, handed it to him and without any sort of segue, dropped him off on the corner of Saint-Laurent and Sainte-Catherine, and told him he'd have to amuse himself, "until tomorrow morning, or the next day." He opened his mouth to protest that, since Moncton, he was having serious abandonment issues, but she cut him off. "You're a big boy. Don't do anything I wouldn't do. *Au revoir,* buddy." And then she drove off, leaving him standing among the tired hookers, the punks and the fans of steamed hot dogs and second-class strip joints.

Olivia smirked as she remembered all the things she shouldn't have done last time she was in Montreal. It had been too long since she'd been back. She'd always thought she'd end up here, living in a wooden-floored, high-ceilinged apartment with more rooms than she knew what to do with, taking walks through Parc Lafontaine at midnight, writing her poems while sitting at terraces on St-Denis and pretending to be sophisticated.

She hadn't written a single word since this damn trip began, and wasn't that the whole damn point? A change of scenery to shake the brain up a bit, open the clogged valves. She wanted to blame it on him, or on the empty Bushmills bottles that rattled in the back of the pickup like the hollow bones of her dead poems, but ultimately it was her own fault. Maybe writing was just the excuse and this trip was about collecting the bits of herself she'd left behind across the country five years earlier. Looking at them one last time, then letting them go like the good Buddhist she was trying to be—sex, booze and smokes notwithstanding.

Driving up boulevard Saint-Laurent, she got stuck in Friday night traffic, which gave her the chance to admire the nymphettes parading up and down the sidewalks, waiting for love to find them—or at least for the doorman of the *club du moment* to let them in. Olivia laughed as she remembered herself in her tight skirts, frilly tops and the knee-high boots she could hardly walk in, absorbing the wolf-whistles and the propositions without batting an eyelash. It was her drug then, all that attention, and French guys sure knew how to give it. She knew now that it didn't amount to much, certainly not love, whatever that was. But she had to admit that the girls in this city knew how to put it on. "The city of beautiful women," a radio host had called it once, and it stuck. Even ugly girls were beautiful here, because they had that *je ne sais quoi*, which translated into sass and style. And down where Olivia had left him, slack-jawed and forlorn, the girls knew how to take it off, too. Anyone could do it, the manager of the Cleopatra assured, if she had the moves and liked it when all eyes were on her. Olivia did. And it had got her the truck, so maybe it hadn't been such a bad thing.

Without thinking, she turned right on Rachel, and rolled all the way to Parc Lafontaine. Its fountain was spurting blood-red arcs of water into the sky, while groups of friends congregated around candlelit picnic tables or stretched out on the grass, enjoying the spectacle, each other, the relief of the summer night. An old man sat alone on a park bench, playing sad music on an accordion for his own pleasure. Olivia wanted to sit next to him, maybe offer him a smoke, but she didn't want to intrude so she just smiled and he nodded his acknowledgement. In the circle where the Félix Leclerc statue stood, a half-dozen drummers were beating out tribal rhythms for an assortment of gyrating dancers. The fountain turned green, and Olivia closed her eyes and joined the dance, raising her hands towards the firmament, shaking out the tensions of the trip, the incident in Quebec City, the past. A young guy, kind of hippie-ish but cute, passed her a fat joint, and she didn't refuse. There was more than one path to enlightenment. Then the water turned into liquid gold shooting in one stream straight up the middle of the fountain. In the distance someone was juggling fire. Olivia gravitated towards the revolving balls of flame. Mesmerized, unstoppable, and finally fully in the moment.

Chapter 8

Alan Cumyn

OTTAWA, ONTARIO

How cold does the wind get on the approach to Ottawa? We were shuddering into an ugly rain, the water on the flat, flat highway assaulting us. Her truck had developed a sickly rattle somewhere in the concrete horrors of Montreal, and water dripped annoyingly through a crack in the windshield. She was snoring in the passenger's seat beside me, her legs splayed open.

She'd been wearing the same jeans since Moncton, and when she found me in the bus station in Montreal I wasn't overjoyed to see her.

"You there!" she'd said to me then, as if the universe was unfolding according to plan. "I thought I might find you here. I want you to show me Ottawa. You said you knew it very well."

"You're late!" I snapped in reply. "I'm heading home. And I have a name, by the way."

Four days I'd been searching for her without a sign.

She looked at me through exhausted, vulnerable eyes. "I was hoping you had one," she said.

Now we drove in silence while arguments built and raged in my head. How could I care anything for this flip of a woman who could love me so passionately one night then abandon me the next? Who couldn't seem to realize when she was thinking and when she was talking out loud? Her leg brushed the gearshift and I pushed it off too harshly. I'd never hit a woman in my life, but this one . . .

This one murmured in her sleep and chewed her lip and could turn from a cold front to heaven's garden in a heartbeat. This one went from sandpaper on the nerve endings to warm oil along the softest skin. This one could wear a man like a pair of best-loved shoes until holes had breached the sole and split the foot.

I kept on driving, but wished I'd made it onto the bus before she'd found me.

She woke up finally when I brought the complaining truck to a halt. She looked as if she was emerging from a mile-deep dive.

"What's this?" she asked.

I wasn't sure if I wanted to take her in my arms or kick her out of the vehicle.

"I thought you were going to show me Ottawa?" she said.

"Here it is," I said. Now that the engine was shut off the silence seemed to press in on us from every direction.

She looked around in confusion. "Where's Parliament Hill?" she asked. "The Art Gallery? The Market? The Château Laurier? Where's the Canal? Where does Adrienne Clarkson live with that husband who has too many names?"

"I thought you didn't want to be a tourist," I said.

I convinced her to get out and walk with me. The place was deserted of course. It generally is.

"This is the heart of the nation's capital," I said after we'd walked for a time along the trail that turned into a boardwalk.

"It looks like—"

"Yes, that's right," I said. "It's a peat bog. The Mer Bleu. It's famous in Ottawa. At least among those who know about it."

"It looks like the tundra," she said, and I saw her whole body relax. She closed her eyes for a moment. "We could be anywhere. Way up north," she sighed. "We could be in Labrador."

We gazed in silence at the tamaracks, the mosses, the

huddled, rounded bushes in a thousand shades of russet, brown and grey that in a trick of the eye seemed to stretch on to the end of the world.

"This is where the great ideas, debates, propositions of the country come to settle and ferment," I said. "Not Parliament Hill, which is just where the politicians eat lunch. Everything looks so still and peaceful here, so clogged and sedentary and unchanging. But every so often something bubbles out of the slime and establishes itself."

She checked her pockets then looked at me, I knew, with the eyes of one about to bum a cigarette. I shrugged my shoulders—none left.

"So this is where compromises are made?" she asked archly.

"I suppose. Yes."

"Bruce," she said, and ran her hand through her hair. "I think I may be pregnant."

Somewhere in the distance a hawk screamed and I fell off the boardwalk.

Chapter 9

Helen Humphreys

KINGSTON, ONTARIO

O livia wasn't pregnant. It was a false alarm.

"I need a break," she said to Bruce, meaning the road trip, meaning him.

They got in the truck and headed south towards Kingston. The last time Olivia had been to Kingston there had been a billboard on the highway approach that had promised, "Kingston—You'll Be Amazed!" She was glad to discover that the sign was gone. It had alarmed rather than excited her.

Amazement was the last thing she wanted from a destination.

For a small town it was extraordinarily difficult to find a parking space, but finally Olivia managed to squeeze the truck between two Hondas on Brock Street.

"Time to spend some time apart," she said to Bruce, as he opened the door and got out of the truck; and she left him there, on the sidewalk, in front of the pet store.

It was Frosh Week in Kingston. All the students were dyed purple, gathered in colourful knots outside the university buildings and in the city parks.

Olivia had always found it intriguing that the two main institutions of Kingston were the university and the prison. The ex-criminals were as easy to spot as the purple students. They zipped around on ten-speeds, lanky, scowling men who had lost their driver's licences and were now forced to ride bicycles, unwillingly getting healthier with every irritable mile. There were around fifty prisoners released onto the streets of Kingston every day and Olivia could spot them right away. They wandered uneasily down Princess Street near the A & P, looking a little bewildered and sporting bad haircuts from the 1970s.

Having walked up Princess Street and through the university grounds, Olivia headed for the lake and wandered along the path that followed the shoreline—past the heavy cannons pointed at America, the helicopter landing pad for the hospital, and a truly atrocious public sculpture of two giant green tubes framing what looked like a puddle of vomit. There were sailboats on the water and a small tour boat that resembled a wedding cake, hurtling with great speed up the lake. It felt good to Olivia to be walking around in the cool September air—and it felt good to be away from Bruce.

Bruce meanwhile was thinking about love. He had thought about love all afternoon and through a lonely dinner of fish and chips at the Pilot House. He had thought about love, but he had reached no conclusions. And now, walking the streets of Kingston after dark, he was trapped in what seemed to be some sort of bizarre theatrical. Everywhere he went there was a group of pudgy, middle-aged people in golf clothes being led about by a university student wearing a black cape and carrying a lantern. There was a group outside the Court House, and another by the church. He finally realized, from overhearing the students talk about bodysnatching and hangings, that this was a ghost walk; and at the same time he decided that love itself was a kind of haunting. You were haunted both by what had been and by what could never be. His trip across Canada with Olivia was becoming his own personal ghost tour.

Bruce and Olivia met up again on the patio of Chez Piggy. They had a beer and eyed one another warily.

"We could end it here," said Olivia.

"Or we could go to Toronto," said Bruce.

Sparrows flitted about the tables in the courtyard, stealing bits of bread and chirping happily.

Bruce still seemed so hopeful. Olivia leaned back in her chair.

"Alright," she said.

Chapter 10

Sheila Heti

TORONTO, ONTARIO

She sat on a bench in the concrete park beside the building, leaned over and scratched her raw ankle. I watched her. I'd had it in my mind that she was headed to Vancouver to visit her brother who huffed glue, but when I brought it up in the middle of the night on the highway she said with irritation that she didn't have a brother.

"Bay and College," she sighed, not looking around. "Have you heard about Bay and College?"

I let out the breath I had been holding in my lungs. "No. There goes Molly Ringwald." I turned my head.

"I'm tired." She continued to scratch.

I had realized by now that I wasn't being fun enough. That I had forced my company on her and hadn't contributed a thing. She probably would have had a better time if I wasn't there. I was determined to make Toronto great, but I had no idea how.

"Come on, let's go to the CNE," I said.

She shook her head.

"Let's go see my friend Matt."

A lady with a wheelbarrow approached us. "Do you have any Canadian literature?" she asked. Olivia looked up, looked at me, then beckoned with her eyes at her knapsack.

"She has an anthology," I said.

The woman reached in, pulled it from Olivia's bag and started to walk away, licking it as she went.

This was making me nervous. "Let's go get really drunk," I said, a bit hyped. "Let's smoke till we fall off our chairs. Let's find some DMT."

She rolled her eyes at me and I slapped her across the face with the edge of my hand. Her face went white and she looked up at me but I just hit her again, impulsively, though this time I didn't mean to, I just felt guilty.

"Monster!" she cried, and got off the bench and ran down the street, tried to cross the road, still running, and nearly got swiped by a car. I should have followed but I didn't know what to say. Truth was, I felt relieved.

Bad about it, but in some basic way, untroubled. I looked around—business people—and though I caught one woman's eye, no one said a thing. It was rush hour. Perhaps no one saw. Now as I looked down the street I couldn't see Olivia. Of course, she wouldn't let me back in the car now. I went off in the direction she had gone, beset by what I'd have to undo, how I would explain. I wanted a drink. When I reached Queen Street, I walked along and found a pub that had a big, crowded patio—the Black Bull it was called—and sat down at a table wedged among all these people talking with their friends. *This goddamn city*, I told myself. *Puts you on edge.* But it wasn't true. I'd almost hit her the night we left Montreal. She'd been snoring in the passenger seat, legs spread on the vinyl. I could never just ruin something a bit. I always had to ruin it completely. I couldn't go back to the car. *That's what happens when you fall for someone impervious to love*, I reasoned. *The bitch*, I reasoned further. I asked a guy at the table next to me for a smoke, but he just shrugged. The waitress still hadn't come. It was like you could do anything in this city and no one would notice, or maybe they were just pretending.

Chapter 11

Uma Parameswaran

WINNIPEG, MANITOBA

Bruce walked out of the platform and into the Via Rail rotunda crowded with people of all colours, many dressed to the nines in ethnic costumes. A woman was holding up a placard that read BRUCE. People around her, waving Canadian flags, chanted in various accents, Bruce Bloos Booze.

"I am Bruce."

"I'm Maru. Sheila sent an enigmatic e-mail from Toronto to say she felt somewhat responsible for some kind of spot she had put you in, and since we writers must stick together, I thought I'd try to help."

"What is this? United Nations?" He waved at the crowd.

"I don't know them any more than I know you. You're looking at the new home of the Citizenship Court. There's the Japanese-Canadian judge who has just administered the oath of citizenship to eighty-seven individuals from thirty-three countries." She led him to her minivan.

"So what did you do on the train?"

"Had four long showers," he said, still surly. "What else can one do on the train? And read every brochure and old newspaper there was. I know more about Winnipeg than I ever care to know. Like Richard Gere and J. Lo and the movies being shot here, that this year's Folklorama had 47 pavilions and 521,000 visitors, that the Fringe Festival sold 67,000 tickets, and the Folk Festival in Birds Hill Park in July had 87 concerts."

This guy's attitude was a pain, but Maru was a team player. Writers Unite. "Kira told me you were a prose writer. I can see you stringing out pieces for the travel section with data culled from newspapers and tourist booths. You can add to your notes that the cellphone inventor, Marty Cooper, grew up in Winnipeg."

They drove out on to Main Street. "You've come in the doldrums, when the summer fun is over and the season for everything else, the Royal Winnipeg Ballet, the

Symphony, half-a-dozen theatre companies, hockey, skating etcetera, has not started."

"Doldrums," Bruce moaned, "I have lost the love of my life; we had such great times all the way from St. John's to Toronto and then psst, gone."

"Man or woman?" Maru asked.

"Olivia," he said, "Fair Olivia of Dunhills and Will Oldham, who rose out of the harbour like Venus from the sea. I just slapped her a couple of times, and she took off."

Maru stopped the car. "You slapped a woman!!! Get out of my car this minute."

Cars behind them honked impatiently. "Okay, okay, for every sin there is an atonement," and she turned right, into the Forks, and walked him to the rivers.

"Here's the confluence of the Red and the Assiniboine," she said, "and confluences are sacred, especially for atonements, 'prayaschittam' it is called in Sanskrit." She tripped him with her left foot, and to be doubly sure simultaneously pushed him, into the river. "Now you are somewhat cleansed," she said, and steered him to the aboriginal circle of sharing so he could dry off on the hot slabs.

"She could be anywhere."

"Let's start with downtown."

She gave a guided tour—from the University of Winnipeg to the strip between the Bay and Eaton's, even though Eaton's had now been razed to the ground to make way for the new arena; to the corner of Portage and Main, the coldest city intersection in the world; the theatre district with its three theatres and the Museum of Man and Nature, now renamed to be gender neutral. Then over the bridge into St. Boniface, to see the Franco-Manitobain Centre, and the Cathedral which had reared its twin towers and circular stained glass window before the fire of 1968. They came back downtown to salute Louis Riel on the Legislature grounds, and atop the dome, the recently regilded Golden Boy who now faced north instead of west.

At Osborne Village, they stopped for dinner. Bruce went on and on about Olivia's imperviousness to love.

"Let's use some logic as to where Olivia might be. A poet-pilgrim might go to Carol Shields' apartment block on Wellington Crescent or to Gabrielle Roy's house, or Margaret Laurence's in Neepawa."

"No, no dead writers."

"Birds? We have Oak Hammock Marsh that has 296 species of birds. Flowers? English Garden and the Conservatory. Statues? The Leo Mol Sculpture Garden, a must-see for every visitor."

"Definitely not the sculpture type."

"With her Zen Buddhist leanings and your slaps, maybe she's decided animals are better company and is with Limba the elephant at the zoo."

At which Bruce hit his head against the table and moaned, "Slaps! What got into me?"

Maru left him at Collective Cabaret to drown his sorrows. "Olivia, only Olivia," he moaned.

Next morning, though she allowed much for writers' excesses, Maru decided enough was enough. He should meet some real people who worked hard at their art—like her tennis friend Yvette who gave piano lessons, or Helma who lived at Winnipeg Beach.

She said they could also go to Gimli, which in the 1950s had been the oolala weekend partying spot for people who came by train from the city. He could write a piece on that. Maybe the replica of the pioneer ship was still there at the harbour. At the word, Bruce came to life. A harbour in the middle of the prairies, hallelujah. First some art and a hardworking artist, Maru said, and he groaned. Helma's studio was full of her own oils and watercolours of long-legged birds, and works by neighbouring artists who lived year-round in little houses along the lake.

As they came out of the house that Helma's partner had just renovated and that Helma dreamed they could rent out next summer, Bruce shouted, "There she is, there she is," and sprinted to a parked GMC with no one in it.

Chapter 12

Arthur Slade

SASKATOON, SASKATCHEWAN

"I am in love," Olivia whispered, her hands tight on the wheel, fighting against the crumbling Yellowhead highway. Ahead lay the horizon, ruler straight, inviting infinity. The sky nestled around them. "I am in love, love, love—head over heels, in fact. I finally know what true love feels like."

Bruce sucked in his breath. Here on the semi-bald prairie she was returning his love. Even after the slaps. This woman, hard as a wheat kernel, had softened under his gushing supplications. He clutched at his heart and felt something hard—ever since Montreal he had been wearing the Oldham CD on a chain around his neck as a symbol of their unity. "I don't know what to say," he said. "I'm in love, too."

She brushed a lock of hair from her forehead. "It's amazing, isn't it? So big, so overwhelming, grandly simple, yet absolutely complicated. And so blue."

"Uh, yeah. Blue." She had lost him there, then he remembered she was a poet. They saw things differently. Even love could be blue to a poet.

"Yes," Olivia said. "For the first time in my life I am completely and madly in love. With the Saskatchewan sky."

Bruce slumped. "Of course. It figures." For the first time in his life he was jealous of the air itself. The sky, as blue as Roy Romanow's eyes, was stealing her away.

"Quick," Olivia said, "hand me my notepad." She began to write while she was driving, using the steering wheel as a desk. "Hold the wheel," she commanded.

He did so, and she stepped on the gas, speeding up with each scribbled word. His hand grew slick as Spam. They passed a graveyard and he wondered how many motorists lay buried there.

Olivia set down her pen, took back the wheel with one hand and held her poem with the other. She read it breathlessly:

"The sky blue

Skeleton requirements of earth and air
Blue above
Blue everywhere."

Bruce chuckled. "I think you're channelling W.O. Mitchell."

"Don't bring me down, Bruce. This is just a first draft. My inner self is awakening. I'll finally be able to write."

They drove. The sky furrowed its brow, turned dark and rumbled in Diefenbaker tones, attacking their truck with hail as though they were the Mackenzie King Liberals. "We'll have to find shelter," she said, as they chugged into Saskatoon and turned right on Eighth Street. The Co-op sign glowed in simple white and red, beckoning them. "My muse needs food."

He followed her inside the grocery store. Men in baseball caps and lumberjack shirts turned their eyes away from thick steaks and frozen hamburger to watch Olivia.

"We have to be careful," Bruce said, putting a bag of beef slices into the cart. "People here have long memories. They're still mad about losing the Riel Rebellion. And don't make fun of the Roughriders."

"Wow, look at these cucumbers! Tomatoes! Cobs of corn! It's wonderful." She stepped towards the plastic bag dispenser. A man in a suit tore a bag off and handed it to her. "Oh my God, they're polite here. Watch."

She reached for another bag, but an elderly lady, head clad in curlers, ripped one off and offered it to Olivia.

"We better get out," Bruce said. "It's immoral to be so polite. They want something. They'll expect us to join the NDP."

With three bags full, they left the store, squeezed themselves back into the truck and drove. They crossed the Broadway Bridge, parking near the Delta Bessborough. They strolled along the South Saskatchewan riverbank, wandered over the Victoria Bridge and tread on land where the Temperance Colonists, founders of Saskatoon, had once set up their tents. Bruce felt ghostly, judging eyes watch his every move. "I gave up cigarettes," he whispered to them, "and booze. Forever."

Olivia, oblivious as always, dropped her blue-jeaned derriere onto a park bench and dug into their groceries. "I could live here. City of bridges. Always a way to the other side. I like that feeling."

"What would you do for money? There aren't any strip clubs."

"I'd write poetry! They worship poets here. It would be the perfect place to raise our child."

For the second time that day Bruce felt his heart stop. "Our child?"

"Yes, Bruce," Olivia spoke easily, as though she were

discussing the weather, "I'm pregnant again and this time it's for sure."

The breeze that followed her words was as warm and healing as Tommy Douglas's breath.

Chapter 13

Dianne Warren

REGINA, SASKATCHEWAN

There's a man who stands every day along the highway just north of Regina. He waves at the people going south into the city and records their responses in a notebook. His system is simple, a checklist with two columns: waved, didn't wave. The people who travel this road daily are used to him, and they sometimes pull over onto the shoulder to hand him a coffee or a Coke or perhaps an egg salad sandwich. He's a constant, like the wind, or the soft gold colour of the wheat field out of which the city rises. The local newspaper once did a feature article on him, although it wasn't very revealing as this is a man who doesn't like to talk about himself. He wouldn't, for example, tell the reporter whether or not there was some traumatic event in his past that had to do with highways, or whether, perhaps, he was on medication. The man would only say, "I treat it as a job, regular hours. I just love it out here."

People who are new to this highway notice the man, but he stays in their thoughts for only as long as he can be seen in their rearview mirror. They think he must want something, but they're confused because he doesn't have his thumb out, he's not holding up a sign, there's no broken-down car anywhere in sight. They sometimes see the notebook in his hand, but it doesn't register. It's the sort of detail you need to see more than once in order to speculate on its purpose. They're more apt to notice the colour of his jacket (red, in spring and fall; yellow on a rainy day; bright blue in winter), which really has not much significance at all.

On a certain day in September, at about the time that Bruce and Olivia (for whom, let's face it, we don't hold out much hope) are leaving Saskatoon, the man's wife drops him off on the edge of the highway. He kisses her, a peck on the cheek through the open window, and then she continues on into the city to work. It's surprisingly warm for this time of year. The man takes his notebook and pen from the pocket of his jacket (red), then removes the jacket and lays it on the ground beside him, along with his thermos of hot tea. When he's organized, he begins to wave and record with the diligence of a biologist observing, say, burrowing owls.

At about noon, he sees a vehicle (let's call it a vehicle so we don't get into problems with continuity) coming into his line of vision. He concentrates, knowing how quickly the vehicle will approach, how little time there will be before it passes. He makes the transition between watching the vehicle and distinguishing its passengers, shadowy at first, and then he sees clearly the two people, a man and a woman, and he waves.

Bruce and Olivia, of course.

They ignore him. They stare straight ahead, stunned, not talking, just travelling south and eventually turning onto the city bypass to reach the Number One Highway West. The man is disappointed but not surprised. He's realistic about his job. How can he know what profound thing has happened to these two between the time they left Saskatoon and now? *They* don't even know what's happened. They are two deer caught in the headlights of pending responsibility, two lovers who, let's face it, don't know the meaning of the word love.

The man checks "didn't wave," and then waits for the next vehicle.

Chapter 14

Thomas Wharton

EDMONTON, ALBERTA

What's the point anymore? Olivia said, slamming on the brakes. Everyone knows the story's over by the time it crosses the Ontario border.

We were in Edmonton. The busy four-lane freeway that had been heading straight for the heart of the city had suddenly turned into a winding gravel track that plunged us down through a forest to the river's edge.

That's the election, I said. The story is something different.

We looked at the olive-drab river, at the trees turning

gold. A peregrine falcon landed on the roof of the truck, gave us a stern look and flapped away. Neither of us said anything. We were both going to act like we hadn't seen it. Why did things have to be that way?

This is a city of storytellers, I said, remembering, and then I knew what I had to do.

You've been here before, Olivia said.

I was born here, I said. There was so much I hadn't told her.

I have to find a storyteller, I said.

We got back in the truck and drove. Up Wayne Gretzky Drive, and down Candy Cane Lane. We passed the wind-chime sculpture that no one can hear because they put it on the busiest street corner in the city. We crossed the High Level Bridge and I finally spotted my storyteller in Old Strathcona. He was coming along Whyte Ave. at a fair clip with his white cane tapping the pavement. He still had that ponytail, probably the last ponytail in the western hemisphere, but how was he going to know that.

Olivia didn't want to meet any of my old buddies. She ducked into Athabasca Books to browse. I hailed the storyteller outside Hub Cigar and Newsstand.

Hey, Bill, I said. It's Bruce.

Hey, Bruce, Bill said. Or is it Evelyn.

It's Bruce, for now. Listen, Bill, I need a story. I need a story real bad.

Oh, boy, Bill said, and he sighed wearily.

Here's one I heard recently, he said. It's about two people, two story-crossed lovers, and a pickup truck. These two people are driving and driving. They're really messed up. They don't know who they are, they don't know where they're going. All they know is that Destiny is gonna get them there, wherever *there* is. But they're wrong. They won't get anywhere until they give up on Destiny. Until they ditch Destiny and there's only the road, scary as freedom.

Thanks, Bill, I said. I understand.

You do? Bill grinned. Good. I wish I did.

I met up with Olivia. She had an armload of Alberta writers. I asked her if I could drive, and she said yes. I drove west. I drove until I found a field where a quorum of cows was grazing. Across the road from the field was West Edmonton Mall. I parked and we both got out of the truck.

There's something I have to tell you about me, I said. But first we have to ditch Destiny.

Olivia nodded, resigned. I think she'd felt it coming in the trickster wind.

Save your secret for the next town, she said. She opened the locker in the box of the truck and lifted out a shotgun and a spade. She loaded the shotgun clumsily. She was crying now.

We have to do it right, she said. We have to give her a decent death and burial.

What do you mean? I said.

I never liked guns. If a gun shows up in a story, you know it's going to go off.

Olivia handed me the shotgun, and nodded towards the pickup truck.

Shoot, shovel, and shut up, she said.

Chapter 15

paulo da costa

CALGARY, ALBERTA

The car screeched and slid to a stop on the loose gravel of Glenmore Reservoir's parking lot.

"Aren't you glad we slipped through the tentacles of suburbia and missed the downtown maze for this?" Bruce stepped out of the truck glad his eyes had stopped colliding against licence plates, billboards advertising cookbooks with a fill-up, housing developments *with a view*. He stretched his bones and yawned loudly. His coyote yawn.

Olivia laughed, "Yeah . . . Calgary, a city on the run, galloping towards the Rockies." She rubbed her arms and legs vigorously, waking up the blood in her limbs. She stretched her eyes across the vast body of water at the heart of the city. She stared west, mesmerized by the glow of the lowering sun touching the first dust of September snow on the Great Divide.

"Come on, let's go down into the woods and bury this mess."

Olivia walked around the truck and gave him the crumpled and extra-large donut box, wrapped in newspaper. He looked over his shoulder. Joggers or dog walkers were too self-absorbed to notice. Good. Invisibility, the best thing about a city, Bruce thought. But in the end it had been an accident. He had purposefully aimed to miss.

Unfortunately, he had forgotten the world was round. Something, someone always ends up getting it in the end. Meanwhile Destiny was still free, plotting, manipulating and controlling. Bruce continued to look over his shoulder.

"We lost the shovel. Maybe we should do this another time." Bruce added, hopeful. He had been successful in postponing the burial since Edmonton. He even purposefully lost the shovel after the toilet stop at the drive-in donut shop.

"Naaaa, we won't reach the West Coast if they ever find us with these dead things in the truck," Olivia said, sliding the knapsack over her shoulders. "Got your sleeping bag in your pack?"

Bruce nodded. His face was tense as he stuffed the box in his pack.

They walked down the path through white spruce and willow, across a small bridge where the Elbow River emptied into the artificial lake, and until the trail moved parallel to the water's edge again.

"This is perfect," Olivia said, scrutinizing the pebble beach and the fescue grass edging the forest.

Bruce didn't say a word and sat, leaning against a birch tree, partially gnawed by a beaver. The wood chips scattered at its base provided a soft cushion. The fragrance of freshly chewed wood relaxed him.

"I don't think they should both be buried." Bruce said, thinking he too dreamed of ending his days under the open sky, the fresh air tingling his nostrils. "I think the Canada goose should be tossed in the woods, and only after it gets to be really dark," he added while following a cormorant gliding over the restful surface of the Glenmore Reservoir. Abruptly, the bird dove. Seconds, minutes elapsed before it reappeared. Its spiked head sparkled against the low sun. Bruce detected the scent of a skunk, heard the canto of a red-winged black bird. A mosquito buzzed around his head. He sprayed the last of the citronella on his face. Offered it to Olivia. She looked annoyed.

"It's *one* mosquito. Probably the last one of the season. It won't kill you."

Bruce shrugged.

Circles rippled the surface of the water. A beaver's brown fur appeared near the edge. It paused and sniffed the air. It smelled his strange mix of cologne and citronella and continued to scout the perimeter of its territory.

Bruce was thinking the worse part about the shooting experience was that he had been so intent on not shooting anything, even Destiny, yet in the end he not only killed one but two beings. Only seconds after the shot echoed through the air, he was not surprised to find the Canada goose at his feet. After all it was fall. But the Shooting Star landing on the truck's cab surely startled him. He guessed now that even lead fired into the sky eventually leads to something. He was glad he did not inadvertently shoot down Mars. People might miss something that size in the sky. Plus, a planet like that might have damaged the truck cab too. Olivia would have not been pleased with a dent that size.

Dusk begun to settle down over the sky. The sound of the beaver chewing sent Bruce foraging in his knapsack. He spread avocado and Camembert on whole rye. A slice of tomato topped the sandwich. He cut the sandwich in half and shared it with Olivia.

For the first time in years Bruce sang, "Four strong winds, that blow lonely . . ."

Olivia cringed.

The sky opened in a glitter of fireflies. Bats glided close by and fanned the air with their flight.

"Are you really a poet?" Bruce asked after he had hummed the song for a few minutes, having had forgotten the words.

"Why have I never seen you writing on this trip?"

"Of course, I am a poet. Can't you tell?" Olivia ruffled her dishevelled hair.

"Everyone is either a poet or a terrorist after the sixth beer." Bruce added emphatically.

The scurry of a red squirrel up a white birch tree echoed in the stillness of the closing day. A twig broke. Sounds came and went with suddenness.

Olivia crouched at the lake's shore, and fantasized about retiring in the country. Olivia fluffed her sleeping bag and curled up inside.

"When I wake up in the morning I don't want to see that box."

Inside his sleeping bag, staring at the sky, he recognized the Little Dipper emptying into the Big Dipper and followed the bottom stars of the bowl pointing towards Castor. He was beginning to doze, listening to the soothing gnawing of the industrious beaver, when he sensed Olivia's body sliding closer to his.

"So, about that secret of yours . . ." Olivia whispered in his year.

A tree fell in the forest.

Chapter 16

Richard Van Camp

FORT SMITH, NORTHWEST TERRITORIES

Bruce listened to the Slave River Rapids as he held a copy of this week's *Slave River Journal* and read a pamphlet highlighting the beauty of Fort Smith. The mayor, Peter Martselos, was about the friendliest man Bruce and Olivia had ever met. Not only that, but he presented them with a copy of Leslie Leong's book of photography and prose titled *Our Forgotten North*, two books of poetry by local poet Jim Green, and a CD called *Lateral Lightning* by local band The Electric Chair Skeletons.

The mayor had told them that this town of 2,500

was a place of stories and rich history and it was also the friendliest place in all of Canada.

"Of all the seasons here on the sixtieth parallel," the mayor continued, "fall is my favourite."

"Why's that?" Bruce asked as he pinned a Town of Fort Smith pin into his shirt.

The mayor smiled and pointed to the sky. "Fort Smith is the third-best place in the world to see the northern lights and they come out so early now. You'll see. Also, now that that summer's over, the bugs are all gone. Now, please excuse me. I have a meeting. Enjoy your day."

Olivia stretched on the lush green lawn by the Mary Kaeser Library until her hip, shoulder and left knee popped. "Ahhh," she sighed. "Now I'm centred."

This was a town of flowers, she thought: pansies, poppies, peonies, tulips and daisies gracing the lawns and flower baskets hanging from every light post downtown. It did say "Garden Capital of the North" on the sign outside of town and she believed it. Fort Smithers were green thumbs, apparently, as there were gardens and greenhouses in every third yard.

Olivia breathed deep and listened to the rapids. She didn't know where they were but she could hear them: relentless with the sound of forever. She looked up and saw a fleet of large white birds soaring together in the sky, weightless against the blue, not flapping their wings at all. They weren't Canada geese. They weren't herons. They were pelicans!

Olivia watched them and ran her hands over her tummy. She thought of her baby—their baby—growing inside of her, using every moment with instinct to grow. Olivia closed her eyes and smiled and thought of the pelicans blessing the sky they flew through and used the sound of the rapids to whisper, "My child, I put these memories in you."

Bruce looked at the pickup's spiderwebbed windshield and shook his head. It had been a seventeen-hour drive from Calgary to Fort Smith. The road was okay, but every time a truck passed them, a rock shot up and nicked the windshield. Three little nicks in the glass had now spread like the palms of spiderwebs reaching out for one other.

"Those will only get worse," he thought, "with every little bump in our way."

The land that led them towards Fort Smith was gorgeous, mostly pine and spruce. They'd seen a herd of twenty-three bison on the outskirts of town that watched them pass warily. The bison were huge animals, giants, and luckily, had let them by without challenge or charge. The drive had been long and Olivia slept most of the way.

Bruce loved to drive but started thinking, "Why did I hit her? Why? And now she's pregnant. Make it up to her, Bruce. Make the rest of her life a garden."

His secret was simple, why he hit her was simple: he feared her. He knew she was stronger than him in every way. Worse, if he pissed her off enough, she could probably kick his ass. "She could lead me," he admitted to himself, "and I'd follow her anywhere."

Now, as Olivia stretched in front of him, Bruce admired her beauty. She was the tallest woman he'd ever been with, and he liked that a lot. She was like climbing a mountain, he thought. She met him face on when they kissed and she kissed with strength. He also loved how her body met his, tummy to tummy. "This could work," he thought. "Make this work."

Bruce watched Olivia reach out to the sky, as if gathering the blue and pulling it into her spirit. Bruce loved the way Olivia's shirt rose, revealing her tanned skin underneath, that smooth skin of hers and his palms ached to touch her. He remembered a line he'd read in the *Edmonton Journal* before they left. The article had a list of the top ten corniest pick-up lines (so far) recorded in Alberta and Bruce recited one that he thought was actually quite brilliant: "You with all those curves, and me with no brakes."

Olivia burst out laughing and turned to him. "What?"

Bruce blushed. "Did I say that with my inside voice or my outside voice?"

She shook her head. "Outside voice."

Bruce smiled. "I'm not sorry you heard that."

Olivia looked at him and smiled. "Tell me about this place."

Bruce felt himself blossom in tingles. There it was again, he thought. There was that lovin' feeling. Look at me: busted windshield and a bun in the oven, and here I am bursting at the seems with joy." He then started to do a little jig. He'd seen people jig on *The Tommy Hunter Show* on CBC when he was a kid and now that he was in the Metis Capital of the North, he couldn't help himself.

Olivia laughed out loud. "What are you doing—a little soft-shoe to start the day?"

Bruce tried to tap dance and burst out laughing. "Well, it says here Fort Smith is officially quadrilingual. They have French, Cree, Chipewyan and English everywhere. It's also the jigging capital of the North."

Olivia sensed, turned and saw the old man first.

An old, old Indian with dark glasses and a cap walked slowly towards them. Unlike the Crees of Alberta, this Dene elder did not have long hair. His hair was short, his hands small. He was wearing black pants and a blue long-sleeved shirt. He wore moccasins protected by black moccasin rubbers and he was slim. The elder walked with an old cane and was smiling, enjoying the day.

"Hello!" Olivia called out.

The elder smiled and walked towards them, holding out his hand. "Tansi."

Olivia took the old man's hand gently and he shook

her hand once, northern style. The old man looked to Bruce but did not offer his hand. "Welcome to Fort Smith," he said to Olivia.

Olivia smiled, "Thank you." This elder was strong, she could tell, old but strong.

"Have you met our mayor yet?" he asked.

"Yes," Olivia said and showed her Town of Fort Smith pin to the old-timer.

"I'm blind," the old man said.

"Oh," she said. "I didn't know. Sorry."

"That's okay," the elder said. "I wasn't born this way. Did the mayor tell you he has a pet fox?"

Olivia smiled at the surprise. "No." She looked to Bruce and was shocked to see that Bruce looked scared—terrified, in fact—of the old man.

"My name is Olivia," she said. "My friend is Bruce. You are?"

The old man looked down, smiled, and passed his hand over her tummy. "You're going to have a girl," he said gently, "and that's a good thing. They say that when a woman gives birth to a girl, that girl becomes her father's greatest teacher." The old man looked at Bruce and stopped smiling.

Something huge was happening here and Bruce didn't like it at all. His right palm—the palm that had struck Olivia's face twice began to burn. Bruce suddenly felt weak and wanted to run. He wanted to find those rapids and dive in, cleanse himself of how filthy he suddenly felt.

The elder spoke firmly to Bruce as if speaking to a child who'd done wrong. "I am happy for you, Olivia, because I see a man who has a lot of learning to do. Now tell her your secret, Bruce."

Chapter 17

Ivan E. Coyote

MCRAE MOTOR INN AND RESTAURANT, JUST SOUTH OF WHITEHORSE, YUKON TERRITORY

Beverly dumped the used coffee grounds into the gar-bage under her work station and put on some fresh. She had seen the headlights scroll like a lighthouse beam across the panelling behind Racheal's head, and had stood up first, carefully putting out her half-smoked menthol, which she would relight and finish later.

"I'll get these two, sweetie," she whispered, exhaling. "You keep studying."

Racheal, the younger of the two by three decades,

had nodded, and let Beverly grab two menus and the ice-water jug and usher the couple to a booth by the window.

"Excellent view of the gravel lot and gas pumps." Beverly joked idly, but neither of them cracked a smile, the girl didn't even look up.

"I'll be right back with some fresh coffee." This got her a weak nod from the guy. He was skinny with random chest hairs curling over the lapels of his jean jacket. His hands looked unnaturally soft to Beverly, like he should be wearing a suit and tie, but wasn't.

On her way back with the coffee pot she checked out what they were driving: shitbox pickup truck with New-foundland plates. Long drive, especially in a piece of crap like that.

Beverly took their orders, passed the yellow slip to Lenny in the back, and resumed her seat across from Racheal and her Sociology textbooks.

"Okay then, so tell me all about them." Racheal put down her pen and stole a smoke from Bev's pack.

Beverly made the lines in her forehead show.

"What? I'm quitting. I'll buy you a pack on the fif-teenth."

"Heard that one before a hundred times." Beverly smiled down at the lipstick end of her menthol. "That's why I smoke these. No one else is supposed to like them."

"Whatever, Bev. So what's the scoop on these two? He looks like a serial killer."

"Well, he thinks he loves her, but he doesn't have the first clue what that means. Watch how he watches everyone watch her. He thinks she's a belonging. Not a serial killer, but wife beater, maybe. Jealous type. The truck is hers, for sure, no guy would have a pink rabbit's foot key chain, not in Newfoundland, anyways."

"How do you know they're from Newfoundland? Accents?"

"License plates, Racheal, have you learned nothing? What are they teaching you up there on that hill? You could learn more here from me, and get paid. Plus all the free cigarettes you can smoke."

Racheal made a get-on-with-it motion with a home-manicured hand.

"Okay, where was I? Oh yeah, well maybe she lives in Newfoundland now, but I think she grew up in Vancouver, or Toronto maybe. Some place big. She asked me if the orange juice was fresh-squeezed."

Both women laughed at that for a minute.

"Plus she wanted her mayo on the side."

Racheal rolled her eyes. "What else?"

"They're on their way out of town. Parked facing south."

A bell dinged from the back and Bev heaved herself to her feet. She balanced his burger in the crook of her left arm, grabbed the girl's sandwich and soup with the same hand, and picked up the coffee pot with her free hand as

she breezed past her work station. She had always been good at this.

The girl was trying to keep her voice down but couldn't. Bev could hear her from five tables away, even over the diesel truck idling on the other side of their window.

"A twelve-year-old son, Bruce? You couldn't just tell me? We had to drive the Alaska-fucking-Highway so you could introduce me to some rug rat of yours that you barely even know?"

Beverly carefully placed their plates in front of them, and slipped the bill under the sugar dispenser, so she wouldn't have to interrupt them again.

She went out into the dusty hallway to phone Reba, who was probably sitting out on their deck watching the moon come up over Tagish Lake. She would tell Reba things were slow tonight, that she would probably be home kind of early. She would tell her to light the candles and put on a clean white dress shirt.

Now that, Beverly thought as she watched the couple eat methodically, without meeting each other's eyes, is what love is. Reba answered on the second ring.

"Hi, baby, it's me. Do we still have that bottle of wine the boys brought over?"

Chapter 18

Steven Galloway

VANCOUVER, BRITISH COLUMBIA

I'm confused, Olivia thought. And who wouldn't be. You meet a guy, misplace an attraction for whales, get slapped, think you're pregnant, find out you're not, then change your mind and decide you in fact are, which is confirmed by a omniscient blind Indian, and all the while you can't help but feel you're acting strangely.

She sighed with the kind of pitiful ferocity only a person who considers themselves a poet can muster. "We're at a point," she said to Bruce, "where something has to happen."

"What?" Bruce was staring intently through the glass of the jukebox. Each table at the diner had a small console that connected to a main unit in the back. A quarter bought you a song. G5—Starship, "We Built This City (On Rock and Roll)." Bruce couldn't say for sure why he liked this song so much. He was uncertain what he thought about a city that was built on rock and roll. He supposed such a city would be an exciting place, and that a lot would happen there, but he also felt that after awhile almost anyone would get tired of it all, and would start to crave a little quiet time. He didn't imagine that there was a lot of quiet to be had in such a city.

Bruce looked out the window, through the drizzling rain and across the street, at a man who was walking four wiener dogs, each of them on a string tied to one leash. There was no way that Vancouver was a city built on rock and roll, and this comforted him greatly, which surprised him.

"Are you even listening?" Olivia asked, the tone of her voice snapping him back to reality in a way he did not appreciate.

"I'm not as young as I used to be."

"This, right here, is a perfect example of what I'm talking about."

"Sorry." Bruce slumped further into the vinyl booth.

Olivia had never seen him act like this. Defeated. She softened her tone slightly. "I'm sorry about your son."

Bruce shrugged. "It's not your fault." And it wasn't. People move, don't leave forwarding addresses, disappear. It happens all the time. It had never specifically happened to him, but he supposed he was due. He hadn't been much of a father, after all.

"What do you want to do?" Her fingers picked at a chip in her coffee cup.

"Sit here. I want to sit here."

"We have a ferry to catch."

"I don't want to go to Victoria. I want to sit right here."

"Don't be ridiculous. You'll love Victoria. They have a wax museum. There's no wax museum in Vancouver."

Bruce said nothing. He wasn't about to be bribed.

"We can't just sit here. We're having a baby. We're expected in Victoria."

"Don't you understand," Bruce said, his voice suddenly strong, almost loud, "that the only reason I'm in love with you is I know you're utterly incapable of loving me back?"

Olivia flinched, pulling her hands off the table and folding them in her lap. Is that true? she wondered. How would a person even know if such a thing were true? No, she'd know. If she wasn't in love with him it was because she didn't want to be, not because she couldn't be. But the question, the real question, was whether she wanted to be or not. Because after all these miles, she still didn't know.

There's only one way to find out, she thought. She fumbled in her pocket, pulled out a quarter and pushed it across the table.

Bruce stared at her for a second, unsure of what she was doing. Then he picked up the quarter and slipped it into the jukebox. Without looking, he pressed G5.

As the song began to play, a look he had never seen before swept across Olivia's face.

Chapter 19

Bill Gaston

VICTORIA, BRITISH COLUMBIA

"I could use one of those Picaroons," Olivia said, more to herself than to Bruce.

"What's a Picaroons?" he asked.

"One of those beers we had in Fredericton," Olivia told him. "Haven't you been paying attention?"

They were loitering on the granite stones of the Victoria Harbour breakwater, waiting for sunrise. Olivia sat shaking her head, tired of this. She had suffered—well, both of them had suffered—a weird series of moods during this journey, moods that had left them not just inconsistent

but at times downright incoherent. Anyway, she was tired of it. If theirs was a story at all it was a disabled one; it had somehow limped cross-country and Olivia knew it was time to dip its misshapen foot in the Pacific, as it were. In any case it was time for action. What had begun underwater would end underwater. Underwater was where she was going to kill him.

It wasn't just those slaps. She had decided in Vancouver, when he chose that stupid song. At its first simplistic notes his face had bloomed with such idiotic grandeur that she could literally see his old adolescent fantasies swimming around on it. His eyes were silly flowers. His tongue sat puppy-like between his lips. Most hateful of all was the deeper knowledge that her foetus was already much smarter than its father.

Beside her now, in his brand new yellow wetsuit, Bruce sat playing with a broken-off crab claw, poking her, pretending it was a scary appendage. He still hummed that song. Two guys stood nearby, casting for any random Atlantic salmon that may have escaped from a local farm.

Olivia was hot in her wetsuit, a powder-blue maternity model. It hadn't been hard to find. You could find anything here, even a buyer for a truck that lacked a windshield. For wetsuit money she had sold it to the squint-eyed part-owner of a grow-op near the ferry. Maybe he was the kind of squint-eyed fellow who wouldn't notice the lack

of a windshield; or maybe he was the kind of squint-eyed fellow who actively sought non-windshieldness, not wanting to be at a remove from his own velocity as he moved through space. It was hard to tell.

Both Olivia and Bruce agreed that Victoria was identical to St John's, if you added Signal Hill, icebergs, some weather, history and a lively bar culture. Olivia could tell that the politics were more oddly complex here though. The safe-injection site, for instance, had a NO SMOKING sign. It was like Buddhism having quiet sex with Robert's Rules of Order.

In any case, she knew she couldn't stay. Not here. Not with her unborn girl. Olivia thought "girl," not because the old wise man had said it. In her experience of mischievous old wise men, them saying "girl" generally guaranteed "boy," but this wise man had looked so mischievous that his prophecies probably went mischievous full circle, and it was indeed a girl.

The sun came up like a coy lemon, and it was time.

Olivia stood. Bruce stood, too. He took her hand. Well, she had let him peel off that first wetsuit, many miles ago, so she might as well let him hold her hand one last time. They flipper-walked into the chuck without speaking.

Olivia waited till they got past the kelp beds and lingcod nests. The sight of him swimming beside her

strengthened her resolve—in all her years of scuba she had never witnessed a person dog-paddling at fifty feet. He held his head up alertly, looking here and there, as though he'd never seen oblivion before. Olivia unzipped her fanny pack and fingered the sawed-off speargun. It had been too easy to find, too.

Bruce smiled watching her load it and take aim. Olivia aimed and aimed, looking into his eyes. What was the point of this? It would be like shooting a puppy. It would be like shooting moss. What was the point of killing off someone who didn't understand why he was being killed off?

Olivia swore violently, which, underwater, sounded like too many bubbles pushed too quickly through a black pipe. She decided to give him something to understand.

She dropped her speargun and slapped him. Once, twice. Being underwater slaps, they weren't much. The first jarred his mouthpiece, sending up a tiny, unexpected bubble. The second hit his goggles, widening his eyes.

These wide eyes no doubt watched as Olivia's powerful kicks pushed her west, alone, out into the Strait of Juan de Fuca. As she swam, her arms cradled her stomach, in the manner of a saltwater crocodile. She had no plan. She did know that the next land was Japan, or perhaps Hawaii, but her fancies were set more on Newfoundland,

and finding that inside passage, grabbing a ride back on a passing humpback, or an iceberg—she could see plenty of them out there, drifting so heavy-assed just beyond sight.

CONTRIBUTORS

Lesley-Anne Bourne received a BA (Honours) in English and Creative Writing from York University and an MFA in Creative Writing from the University of British Columbia. She has published three books of poetry: *The Story of Pears* (shortlisted for the League of Canadian Poets' first-book award), *Skinny Girls* and *Field Day*. She has won the Air Nova/Milton Acorn Poetry Award and Carl Sentner Fiction Award, and received the 1994 Air Canada/Canadian Authors' Association Award for Canadian writer under thirty with outstanding promise. Her first novel, *The Bubble Star*, was published in 1998. She has been an instructor at the Maritime Writers Workshop and Artsperience.

Herménégilde Chiasson studied visual arts at Mount Allison University, Université de Moncton and New York University, and received his PhD from the Sorbonne. His poetry has won the Governor General's Award and twice

won the Prix France-Acadie. In 1990 the government of France named him a Chevalier des Arts et des Lettres. He has produced some fifteen films, written twenty plays, and exhibited his paintings and photographs in galleries around the world. *Climates*, winner of the Governor General's award, is his latest work in English translation. He is currently Lieutenant-Governor of New Brunswick.

Alan Cumyn is the nationally bestselling author of five novels for adults, including *Man of Bone, Burridge Unbound*—winner of the Ottawa Book Award and shortlisted for the prestigious Giller Prize in 2000—and most recently, *The Sojourn. The Secret Life of Owen Skye* is his first book for young readers. Alan lives with his wife and two daughters in Ottawa.

paulo da costa is a widely published poet, fiction writer and translator. Born in Luanda, Angola, and raised in Portugal, he now calls Canada home and has been, for the last few years, an editor of Calgary's *filling Station* magazine. His debut novel, *The Scent of a Lie*, earned the City of Calgary W.O. Mitchell Book Prize and the Commonwealth Writers Prize for Best First Book, Canada and Caribbean region.

Ivan E. Coyote was born and raised in Whitehorse and now resides in Vancouver with Déjà the husky and Goli-

ath the Pomeranian cross. Her first book of short stories, *Close to Spider Man*, won the Danuta Gleed Award. Her second book, *One Man's Trash*, has garnered international acclaim. Ivan is currently at work on a novel, *the garden*, and *Pee America*, an instructional video for travellers. She performs with One Trick Rodeo, a spoken-word/musical collision.

Tess Fragoulis was born in Heraklion, Crete, and grew up in Montreal, where she currently lives. Her first book, *Stories to Hide from Your Mother*, garnered rave reviews and a nomination from the Quebec Writers' Federation for Best First Book. One of the stories has been adapted for the erotic TV series *Bliss*. In 1983, she returned to her homeland, where she encountered all manner of gods and monsters—who appear in various incarnations in her first novel, *Ariadne's Dream*.

Steven Galloway teaches creative writing at the University of British Columbia. His first novel, *Finnie Walsh*, was shortlisted for the *Books in Canada* First Novel Award. His second novel, *Ascension*, has been published in eight countries and will be serialized on CBC Radio. He lives in Vancouver with his wife, dog and cat.

Bill Gaston grew up in Winnipeg, Toronto and North Vancouver, and has worked as a logger, salmon fishing

guide, group-home worker and as a hockey player in the south of France. His novels include *Bella Combe Journal*, which was a finalist for the Seal Books First Novel Award, *Sex is Red* and *The Good Body*. He has also written plays and published four short story collections, the latest of which, *Mount Appetite*, was nominated for the 2002 Giller Prize. He teaches writing at the University of Victoria.

Sheila Heti's first book, *The Middle Stories*, has been praised by critics from coast to coast. Her work has appeared in such journals as *McSweeney's*, *Toronto Life* and *Blood & Aphorisms*. Sheila studied playwriting at the National Theatre School in Montreal before returning to Toronto, where she lives now.

Helen Humphreys has written three novels, most recently the internationally acclaimed *The Lost Garden*. Her first, *Leaving Earth*, won the City of Toronto Book Award. Her second, *Afterimage*, won the Rogers Writers' Trust Fiction Prize and received brilliant critical reviews both at home and internationally, including a *New York Times* Notable Book listing. Helen is also the author of *Ethel on Fire*, a novella, and is an award-winning poet whose collections include, *Anthem*, *The Perils of Geography* and *Nuns Looking Anxious*. She lives in Kingston.

Mark Anthony Jarman is the author of *Ireland's Eye, 19 Knives, New Orleans is Sinking, Salvage King, Ya!, Dancing Nightly in the Tavern* and a poetry collection, *Killing the Swan*. He has won the MacLean-Hunter Endowment Award for Literary Non-Fiction, a National Magazine Award, and the ReLit Short Fiction Award. Mark's stories and essays have been shortlisted for the Journey Prize, the Pushcart Prize, *Best American Essays*, and the O. Henry Award. He teaches at the University of New Brunswick in Fredericton.

Donna Morrissey was born in The Beaches, a small village on the northwest coast of Newfoundland that had neither roads nor electricity until the 1960s. Her first novel, *Kit's Law*, won the Canadian Booksellers Association First-Time Author of the Year Award. Her two screenplays have won the Atlantic Film Scriptwriting Competition two years in succession, with one of her scripts, *Clothesline Patch*, filmed and aired on CBC. Her second novel, *Downhill Chance*, was a national bestseller. She studied at Memorial University in St. John's and lived in various parts of Canada before settling down in Halifax, where she now lives.

Uma Parameswaran was born in Madras and grew up in Jabalpur, India. Since 1966 she has been living in Winnipeg, where she is a Professor of English at the University of Winnipeg and the current President of the Immigrant

Women's Association of Manitoba. Her first book of fiction, *What Was Always Hers*, won the 1999 New Muse Award and the 2000 Canadian Authors Association Jubilee Award. A novella, *The Sweet Smell of Mother's Milk-Wet Bodice*, appeared in 2001. *Mangoes on the Maple Tree* is her first novel. She has also published books of drama, poetry and *SACLIT: An Introduction to South Asian Canadian Literature*.

Arthur Slade is the author of *Dust*, a national bestseller and the winner of the 2001 Governor General's Award for Children's Literature and the Saskatchewan Book Award for Children's Literature. He is also the author of *Northern Frights*, a series of young adult novels based on Icelandic folktales. Arthur now writes full-time from his home in Saskatoon. His latest, published in 2002, is *Tribes*.

Richard Van Camp is a member of the Dogrib Nation from Fort Smith. A graduate of the En'owkin International School of Writing and the University of Victoria's Creative Writing BFA Program, Richard is currently working on his Master's Degree in Creative Writing at the University of British Columbia. He wrote for CBC's *North of 60* television show for two months and was a script and cultural consultant with them for four seasons. Richard is the author of a novel, *The Lesser Blessed*; a book of short stories, *Angel Wing Splash Pattern*; and two children's books with

artist George Littlechild, *What's the Most Beautiful Thing You Know About Horses?* and *A Man Called Raven*.

Dianne Warren is both a fiction writer and playwright. She won three Saskatchewan Book Awards for her collection of short stories, *Bad Luck Dog*, and was nominated for the Governor General's Award for Drama for her play *Serpent in the Night Sky*. She has won both Western and National Magazine Awards for her fiction. Diane's latest collection of stories is *A Reckless Moon*. She lives in Regina.

Nalini Warriar was born in Kerala, India, and grew up in Assam and Bombay. A molecular biologist, she lived in Germany and France before settling in Canada in 1986. She won the 2002 Quebec Writers' Federation McAuslan First Book Prize for *Blues From the Malabar Coast*. She has a doctorate from Laval University in Quebec City, where she now lives with her husband and their two children. She has completed her first novel, *The Enemy Within*, and is working on her second.

Thomas Wharton was born in Northern Alberta. His acclaimed first novel, *Icefields*, won the Commonwealth Writers Prize for Best First Book (Caribbean and Canada), the Writers Guild of Alberta Best First Book Award and the Banff Mountain Book Festival Grand Prize. *Salamander*, Wharton's bestselling second novel, arose out of his

lifelong love of books and reading. Wharton lives in Edmonton with his wife, Sharon, and their children.

Michael Winter was born in England and grew up in Newfoundland. He has published two short story collections, *One Last Good Look* and *Creaking in Their Skins*, as well as the novel *This All Happened*, which won the Winterset Award and was shortlisted for the Rogers Writers' Trust Fiction Prize. He now divides his time between St. John's and Toronto. His second novel, *The Big Why*, was published in 2004.